MW01690452

RELEASE GOD'S POWER!

EXPERIENCE THE BENEFITS OF PRAYING IN TONGUES

Release God's Power!
Experience the Benefits of Praying in Tongues

ISBN 978-981-14-0458-0

Joseph Prince Resources
www.JosephPrince.com

Printed in the Republic of Singapore
First edition, first print: January 2019

INTRODUCTION

Are you feeling troubled, uncertain, or anxious today? Maybe you're facing a challenge or dealing with a long-term problem that is still not resolved. Perhaps you've prayed about it—diligently—but still feel like you're getting nowhere with the situation.

If that is you, I have good news for you!

God doesn't want you to face your problem alone. He wants to equip and enable you to rise up and walk in His divine power in every situation—through His precious gift of tongues.

Tongues is a heavenly prayer language that will help you to pray effectively according to God's will, and usher in His wisdom and answer for every demand or situation. This powerful grace gift from God will build your faith, repair your body, and cause you to experience His healing, protection, and practical supply in your life. It's one grace gift with many benefits. Best of all, you only have to receive it to start flowing in it.

My heart in writing this book is to encourage those of you who have received tongues but have not been practicing this gift to start praying in tongues again. If you're facing a challenge right now, don't try to handle the situation in your own strength. Instead, get a fresh revelation of this grace gift that God has given you and begin praying in tongues as you rest in God's love for you.

If you have never prayed in tongues, I want to show you from Scripture how this gift applies to you and the powerful benefits of this practical grace gift. Discover how to start praying in this God-given prayer language and trust that the Spirit of God, who understands all your concerns and sees where the problem lies, is able to lead you to victory.

Beloved, I pray that the vital truths and testimonies shared in this book will help you to understand how praying in tongues releases God's solution for any challenge or adversity. May you learn how to flow in this grace gift and experience supernatural breakthroughs!

In His love,

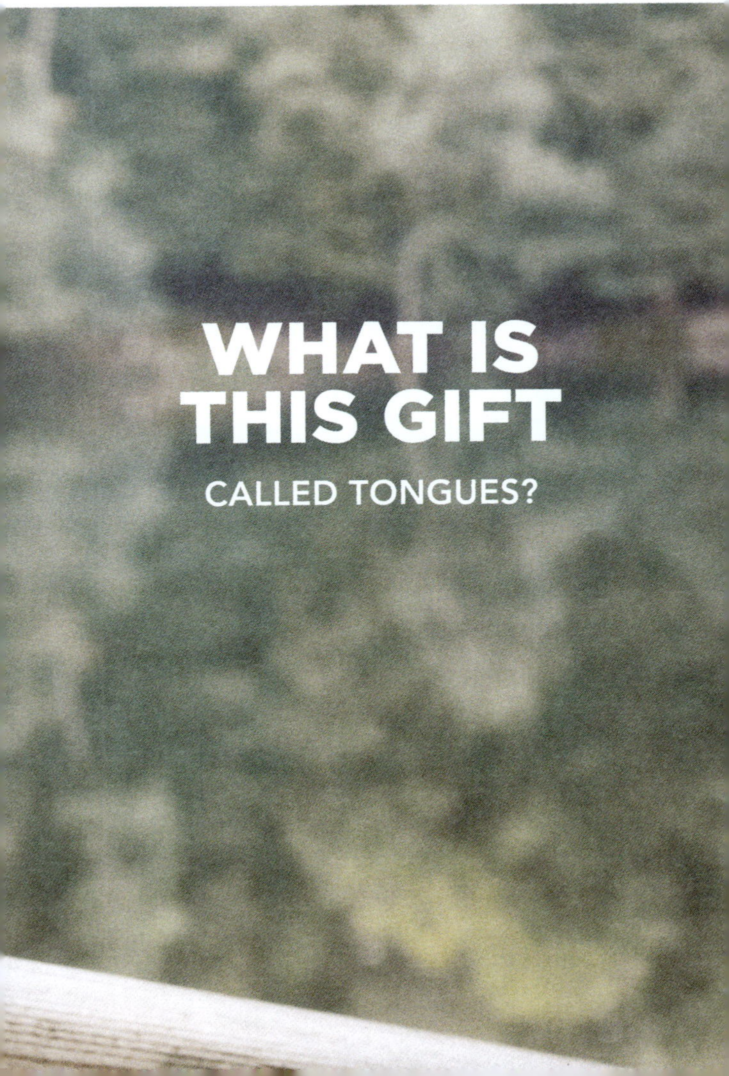

WHAT IS THIS GIFT

CALLED TONGUES?

Tongues is God's amazing gift to His children to help us pray powerful, accurate prayers.

Did you know that God has given you a most wonderful gift by which you can unlock His healing, protection, wisdom, and supply in your daily life?

It is a powerful weapon against the attacks of the enemy, the perfect prayer in every situation, and a divine channel that brings healing and health to your body. This gift is the gift of tongues.

WHAT IS "TONGUES"?

In the New Testament, the apostle Paul shows us how we as believers have been given a very special gift—tongues, the heavenly language of the Holy Spirit. Why is this such an extraordinary gift?

Romans 8:26–28 shows us how the gift of tongues is an immense blessing to our prayer life: When we don't know how to express what's in our hearts to God, or when we don't know what God wants us to pray for, the Holy Spirit prays for us with "groanings that cannot be expressed in words" (NLT).

Isn't it comforting to know that where we may be weak and limited, the Holy Spirit is not, and He is able to pray for us in harmony with God's perfect will? And the result of this? We will see God causing everything to work together for our good and for His glory!

Beloved, tongues (or praying in the Spirit) is God's amazing gift to His children to help us pray powerful, accurate prayers. When you pray in tongues, you will never pray amiss because the Spirit who knows what God's perfect will for us is, is interceding on your behalf. When you pray in tongues, you open the door to let in His power, healing, and practical provision for every need you have.

Jesus likened the Holy Spirit to rivers of living water flowing out of us in John 7:38–39. When you pray in the Spirit, you are activating these rivers of living water—rivers of the Spirit's healing, power, life, and blessings—and allowing them to flow into your situation!

Now does this mean that believers who do not pray in tongues do not have the Holy Spirit?

Certainly not. As a believer, you received the Holy Spirit the moment you made the Lord Jesus your Savior. Through His finished work at the cross, Jesus has made you so clean—so righteous—that the Holy Spirit lives in you today (see 1 Cor. 3:16). This means you can have the Holy Spirit even if you don't pray in tongues.

However, God loves you so much, He wants only the best for you. He gave us tongues so that the Holy Spirit, whom the Bible calls our Helper (see John 14:16), can help us pray effectively and bring God's practical blessings into our lives.

HOW IS TONGUES A GRACE GIFT?

The most encouraging thing about tongues is that it is a grace gift. As a gift, it is something you simply receive; it is not something you work for or earn. Tongues is a grace gift paid for by the blood of Jesus! His work on the cross has made you so righteous that His Holy Spirit abides in you and can't wait to fill you.

The apostle Paul mentions tongues in the list of gifts of the Holy Spirit that God has given the church. If you look up the word "gifts" in 1 Corinthians 12:4, you will realize the word is from the Greek word *charisma* which literally means *gift of divine grace.*

According to Strong's Concordance, tongues is one of God's grace gifts "denoting extraordinary powers… the reception of which is due to the power of divine grace operating on their souls by the Holy Spirit."[1]

Beloved, tongues is God's *grace gift* to you, to empower you and cause you to walk in the supernatural so that His glory can be seen in your life. All you need to do is ask Him for it to receive it. This phenomenal gift will not just change your prayer life, it will touch and change every area of struggle and bring in His victory.

Footnote:

1. NT: 5486, James Strong, *Biblesoft's New Exhaustive Strong's Numbers and Concordance with Expanded Greek-Hebrew Dictionary.* Copyright © 1994, 2003, 2006 Biblesoft, Inc. and International Bible Translators, Inc.

WHY IS TONGUES IMPORTANT

FOR THE BELIEVER TODAY?

Our tongues are the gateway that allow the Lord's blessings to enter our lives.

Is there scriptural evidence that tongues is a gift God wants us, His children, to lay hold of? Absolutely! Before Jesus ascended to heaven, among His final words to His disciples were, *"And these signs will follow those who believe: In My name they will cast out demons; they will speak with new tongues"* (Mark 16:17).

Jesus was telling His disciples that the gift of tongues would be a sign of believers walking in the supernatural power of the Lord. Later, in Acts 1:4–8, just before He was taken up to heaven, we see the Lord commanding His disciples to wait in Jerusalem for the "Promise of the Father"—that they would be baptized with the Holy Spirit with the speaking of tongues, receive power when that happened, and be witnesses to Him.

And indeed, this happened on the Day of Pentecost shortly after (see Acts 2). The account of the amazing events that occurred on that day shows us how the church was born when the 120 disciples in the Upper Room were baptized in the Holy Spirit and spoke in tongues. I want you to notice how the ability to speak in tongues was the very first supernatural gift that God gave to His beloved church:

And suddenly there came a sound from heaven, as of a rushing mighty wind, and it filled the whole house where they were sitting. Then there appeared to them divided tongues, as of fire, and one sat upon each of them. And they were all filled with the Holy Spirit and began to speak with other tongues, as the Spirit gave them utterance.

ACTS 2:2–4

On the Day of Pentecost—the most significant of all days after Jesus' death and resurrection—of all possible gifts, God gave His church the gift of tongues as they were all filled with the Holy Spirit. Do you think God would have given them something that would not benefit them, glorify Christ, or magnify Him?

Just look at the experience of those who heard the disciples speaking in tongues that day. These men, who were from Jerusalem and "every nation under heaven," responded with amazement when they heard the disciples speaking in tongues—*"Look, are not all these who speak Galileans? And how is it that we hear, each in our own language in which we were born?…we hear them speaking in our own tongues the wonderful works of God"* (Acts 2:7–11).

My friend, when you pray in tongues, you are speaking the wonderful works of God! You are not boasting in your own works, but *His* wonderful works. It also tells us that apart from a heavenly language, you could be speaking the Japanese tongue, or Hebrew tongue, or Italian tongue. Like the disciples, you may not know it, but the ones listening to you would hear the wonderful works of God and marvel, giving God the glory.

Can you just imagine how wonderful it would be if we could just speak the wonderful works of God throughout the day? Angels would respond, demons would flee, our minds would come alive, and our spirits, souls, and emotions would be refreshed! We would truly see the power of the Spirit manifesting in our lives and circumstances!

EMBRACED BY THE SPIRIT AND MAGNIFYING GOD

Let me show you one more thing about the moving of the Holy Spirit and the gift of tongues as revealed in the New Testament. Every time the Bible records God's Spirit coming or falling upon believers, it is always accompanied by them speaking in tongues.

Apart from the account in Acts 2, we see this in Acts 10 when Peter preached in the house of Cornelius, a God-fearing Gentile centurion. The Bible says the Christian Jews who had gone with Peter were astonished that the gift of the Holy Spirit was poured upon these Gentiles. (In the Greek, the word used to describe the Holy Spirit falling upon Cornelius' household actually means to *embrace with affection*.[2]) Now, how could they tell this had happened? The Bible says: "for they heard them speak with tongues and magnify God" (see Acts 10:44–46).

Beloved, the Scriptures show us clearly that tongues is a heavenly gift that God wants His beloved children to have. It's a gift by which you can feel the Spirit's embrace, be empowered with supernatural abilities, and magnify the Lord. It's a gift that will take your walk with the Lord to a whole new level!

WHY DOES GOD TOUCH OUR TONGUES?

Why does God give us a gift that touches our *tongues*? My friend, tongues is such an important and practical gift precisely because it touches this small human organ.

The Bible shows us through different visual aids in James 3:2–8 that the tongue, although a little member, is capable of great power. In the same way a bit in a horse's mouth controls the direction it goes, a huge ship is guided by a much smaller rudder, and a spark can set a whole forest on fire, so your tongue can direct the trajectory of your life.

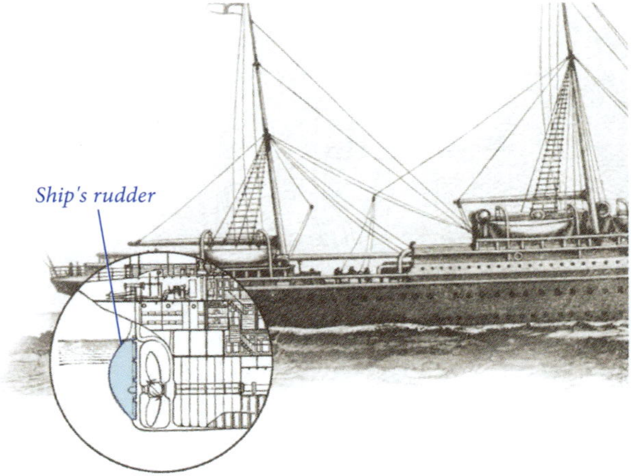

Our tongues are the gateway that allow the Lord's blessings to enter our lives. The Bible tells us plainly that life and death are in the power of the tongue (see Prov. 18:21). God knows that if He can have your tongue, He can turn your whole life around. As you pray in the Spirit and speak in tongues, you allow Him to heal you and touch your circumstances—your financial challenges, your relationships, or that troubling situation in your family or workplace.

Would you like to give the Lord control of your life effortlessly? You can as you receive and begin to walk in His gift of tongues. You'll begin to see how, when He is in control, lack and sickness leave. When He is in control, healing, wisdom, and life reign!

Footnote:

2. NT: 1968, James Strong, *Biblesoft's New Exhaustive Strong's Numbers and Concordance with Expanded Greek-Hebrew Dictionary.* Copyright © 1994, 2003, 2006 Biblesoft, Inc. and International Bible Translators, Inc.

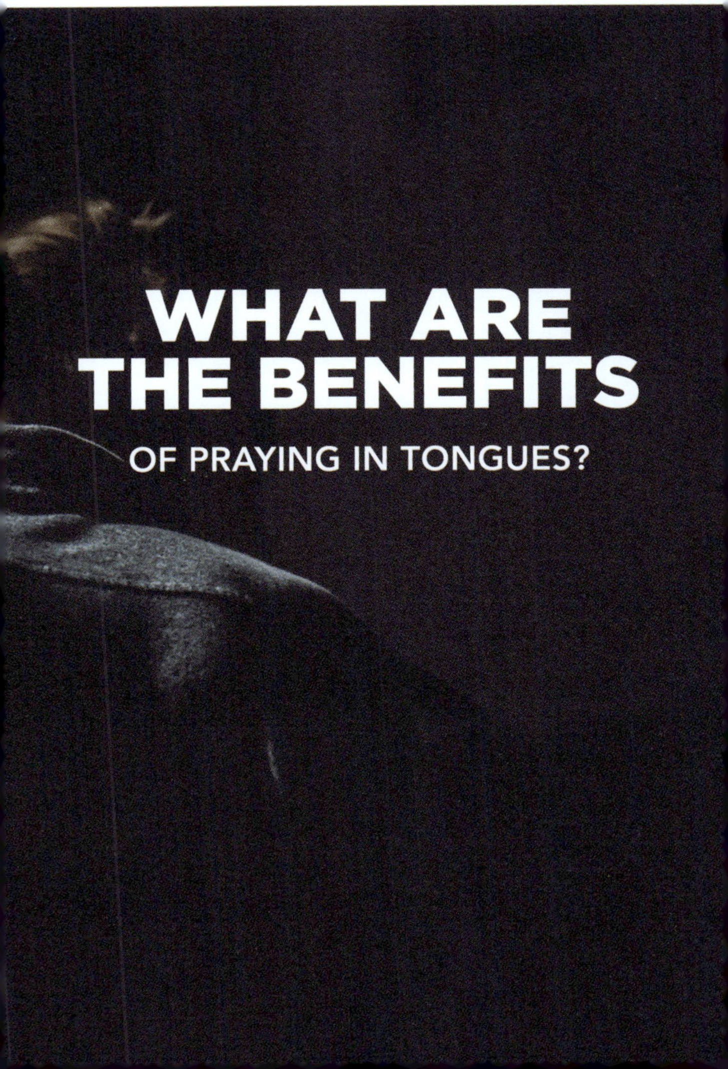

WHAT ARE THE BENEFITS

OF PRAYING IN TONGUES?

When you pray in tongues, you release rivers of God's wisdom, supply, and healing into your situations.

What do you do when you have a need? You talk to God in prayer about it and trust Him to provide for you, don't you?

Now imagine if you had a heavenly prayer language that enables you to always pray perfect prayers in harmony with God's will, which is to bless you with good and perfect gifts (see James 1:17). This includes divine wisdom, the building up of your spirit and your faith, healing for your body, and wholeness for your mind. Praying in tongues gives you access to all these blessings.

This is why God wants you to receive and utilize this powerful grace gift. It's one gift with many applications and benefits!

IT MAKES YOUR PRAYER LIFE POWERFUL AND UNLIMITED

Tongues is a language the Holy Spirit puts inside us to express to God everything we are unable to put into words because of our human limitations. It is a powerful prayer gift not limited by distance, time, or head knowledge.

Often, when we have a problem, we may not know everything about it or how to resolve it. Hence, we may pray with limited knowledge or understanding about the situation. But if you pray in the Holy Spirit, you are allowing Him to intercede for you. And the Spirit, who is not limited, knows *all* things. He knows exactly what the problem is and exactly what you need. He knows how to bring God's best solution into your situation (see Rom. 8:26–27 NLT). He is able to plead for you in harmony with God's will and cause everything to work together for good in every area of your life (see Rom. 8:28)!

Did you know that when you pray in tongues, you could also be prophesying good into your future, or even be praying for the protection of your loved one? Martin from Georgia, who has been following my teachings via broadcast in the US, experienced this firsthand:

"One day, after I came home from work, I felt a strong prompting to pray in the Spirit. Even though I had no idea who the prayer was for, I knew that everything was safe in the Lord's hands.

Later, I received a call no parent would want to get. My daughter, who lives in New Hampshire, had a horrific car accident. According to the state police report, her car had veered off the road at eighty miles per hour and hit a sixty-feet-tall tree. The impact was so great that her car flipped over several times and the engine broke apart.

The accident happened minutes after I prayed. According to my daughter, a state policeman said to her, 'Lady, you should be dead. I've never seen anyone come out of something like this alive!' Praise God that my daughter only sustained minor bruises and a scratch!

I give Jesus all the praise and glory for saving my daughter's life that day! What a wonderful Jesus we serve!"

What an amazing testimony! When you pray in the Spirit, you may not know it, but you could be effectively and supernaturally covering your loved ones or your future with God's protection (while being spared the details that would honestly frighten you). The best part about it is that you can do it as you're pretty much going about your day. You can pray in the Spirit under your breath as you're driving, showering, or attending to any mundane chore… and be praying powerful prayers throughout the day!

IT BUILDS UP YOUR FAITH

Jude 1:20–21 encourages us to pray in tongues because it builds us up on our most holy faith and keeps us in the love of God. When you pray in tongues, you are reminding yourself that God is working in you, for you, and through you. You are fortifying your inner man. You are strengthening your faith, and keeping yourself in the Lord's love for you.

Once, as I was studying the Word, the Lord also showed me an inward vision of how when we pray in tongues, a watery shield goes up around us. We've learned that water is a picture of the Holy Spirit (see John 7:38–39), but why a *shield* of *water*? Because that is how we *quench* all the *fiery* darts of the enemy (see Eph. 6:16).

Imagine being constantly surrounded by this powerful shield as you pray in the Spirit while you go about your day. You don't have to fear the devil's attacks against you. You can go from faith to faith, walking boldly in the promise that no weapon formed against you or your loved ones shall prosper (see Isa. 54:17)!

IT RELEASES RIVERS OF PRACTICAL SUPPLY AND LIFE INTO YOUR SITUATIONS

What is your need today? God has prepared rivers of practical supply to bring healing, life, and provision for all your challenges. As a new covenant believer, you have full access to these rivers of life through the Holy Spirit. When you pray in the Spirit, you release rivers of His wisdom, supply, and healing into your situations.

Are you hard pressed for a decision regarding your family, your job, your relationships, or your finances? Stir up the reservoir of divine wisdom that is dormant on the inside of you, and release rivers of wisdom to bring light and discernment into your situation.

I've found that the more I pray in the Spirit, the more my spirit becomes sensitive to His leading. Similarly, as you practice this gift, you'll become more familiar with sensing the presence or absence of the Lord's peace regarding a matter. And the more you learn to recognize and follow His leading of peace, the more you'll be equipped to make the right decisions, find yourself at the right place at the right time, and experience His protection.

Now, apart from the river of wisdom, there are many other rivers of power that will impart life to your body or circumstances. There is a river of life for a sound mind, a river of love, another river of rest, yet another river of refreshing—all waiting to be released as you pray in the Spirit. Instead of feeling drained and dry of supply, let His living water flow freely as you consistently practice this powerful gift!

IT BRINGS DIVINE HEALING AND HEALTH TO YOUR BODY AND MIND

Praying in tongues is a powerful, scriptural way you can experience healing for both your mind and body. If you have been suffering from a painful physical condition, panic attacks, depression, or some other debilitating medical condition, let me show you how using God's gift of tongues can bring about healing and wholeness to your body and mind.

Look at what the apostle Paul says in 1 Corinthians 14:4—*He who speaks in a tongue edifies himself.*

According to Thayer's Greek Lexicon, the word *edifies* is translated from the Greek word *oikodomeo*, which means "to build a house, erect a building… to restore by building, to rebuild, repair."[3] Isn't that interesting, considering that our physical bodies are the *houses* or *temples* of God's Spirit (see 1 Cor. 6:19)?

And doesn't this tell us that as we pray in tongues, we can rebuild or repair our bodies broken down by age, stress, or disease?

You may have heard that when you pray in tongues you edify or charge up only your spirit or inner man. But 1 Corinthians 14:4 doesn't say that only your inner man is edified. It says that the one who speaks in tongues edifies *himself.* Does *himself* include the person's eyes, ears, nose, kidneys, liver, heart, brain, bones, joints, muscles, nervous system, and every other part of his body? Of course it does!

Beloved, your *entire self*—spirit, soul, *as well as body*—gets edified or rebuilt as you pray in tongues. God takes care of the whole package. So don't limit this restorative effect to just your inner man. Start believing that as you pray in tongues, your body is also getting rejuvenated and repaired.

Perry, a member from my church, wrote to me about how a 29mm cyst found at the head of his pancreas was dramatically reduced in size to 15mm in just two months after he prayed in tongues. As a result, he didn't have to go through a Whipple procedure—an operation more complex than a heart transplant. This is what he shared:

"When my doctor told me the seriousness of my pancreatic condition and how I might have to have the Whipple operation, I became really frightened and prayed to the Lord for healing. I would pray in tongues during my quiet time as you taught us to. This helped to strengthen my faith and remove negative thoughts. I told God I didn't want to go through the Whipple procedure and prayed for the cyst to be reduced in size and to disappear eventually.

When I went for the scheduled check-up, I felt a sense of calm and peace in my heart. I continued to pray in tongues as I waited for the medical report. Lo and behold, the cyst had reduced in size to 15mm! It had shrunk by half in two months! The doctors also found it was benign. As such, I only needed to return once a year for a check-up. What a miracle!

I'm continuing to pray in tongues and believe the cyst will completely disappear by the time of my next visit."

That, my friend, is the power of praying in tongues. Is there an organ in your body that needs repair? A heart that doesn't always beat right, or perhaps an embarrassing skin condition that has defied all the remedies you have tried? Beloved, whether you have been discouraged by a bad medical report, a long-term health condition, or you are suffering from panic attacks and depression, give it all to the Lord and let His Spirit repair and restore your body and mind. God wants you whole in every way, both inside and out!

IT HELPS YOU OVERCOME FEARS

Does fear have a hold on your heart and mind? Perhaps you're imprisoned by the fear of losing something or someone, of falling sick, or of dying. The Bible tells us clearly that fear "involves torment" (1 John 4:18), something that is not part of God's will for His children.

ONLY
THE PERFECT
LOVE OF GOD
CAN CAST OUT
FEAR.

How can the gift of tongues deliver us from the bondage of fear? Earlier, we read how praying in the Spirit keeps us in the love of God (see Jude 1:20–21). In talking about how fear involves torment, the apostle John tells us that only the perfect love of God can cast out fear (see 1 John 4:18). So one of the ways to keep ourselves in the love of God is to pray in the Spirit. And as you do, fear will be driven completely out of your life.

Let me show you another scripture about how tongues can drive out fear. In 2 Timothy 1:6–7, Apostle Paul reminds Timothy:

Therefore I remind you to stir up the gift of God which is in you through the laying on of my hands. For God has not given us a spirit of fear, but of power and of love and of a sound mind.

2 TIMOTHY 1:6–7

In the Greek, the word "gift" here is the word *charisma* which is *grace gift*, the same word describing how tongues is a *gift* of the Spirit (see 1 Cor. 12:4).

Now of all of the gifts of the Spirit, which gift can you stir up at will? I believe Paul is referring to the gift of tongues. Paul was reminding Timothy that stirring up the gift of tongues is key to living free of fear and experiencing power, love, and a sound mind—blessings that are also your inheritance in Christ.

Let me show you how this happened for Nancy from North Carolina. Already baptized in the Holy Spirit, she took special notice when she heard me teach on how praying in tongues could take away our fears and anxieties. That piqued her interest because she had become very fearful of driving in thunder and rainstorms. She told me:

> *"After watching that sermon on tongues, I had the opportunity to pray in tongues through a bad storm while driving. Instead of panicking, I began to pray in tongues before I approached the storm and kept praying in tongues until I had driven out of it. All during that time, I was at total peace with no panic or anxiety. It was amazing!*

I praise God that He brought me through this! I learned to fix my eyes on Jesus as I prayed in tongues and today, I have no more fear of storms!"

If like Nancy, there is something that you are fearful about—it could be your health, children, or future—I encourage you to pray in tongues. As you do, like Nancy, you will find your fears supernaturally replaced by God's love and perfect peace, and experience victory over fear and anxiety.

My friend, whatever your challenge is today, I want you to know God loves you and has already provided all that you need. Tap into His grace gift of tongues and experience rivers of His power, supply, and life for every challenging circumstance today!

Footnote:

3. NT: 3618, James Strong, *Biblesoft's New Exhaustive Strong's Numbers and Concordance with Expanded Greek-Hebrew Dictionary.* Copyright © 1994, 2003, 2006 Biblesoft, Inc. and International Bible Translators, Inc.

HOW CAN I RECEIVE

THIS GIFT AND WALK IN ITS BLESSINGS?

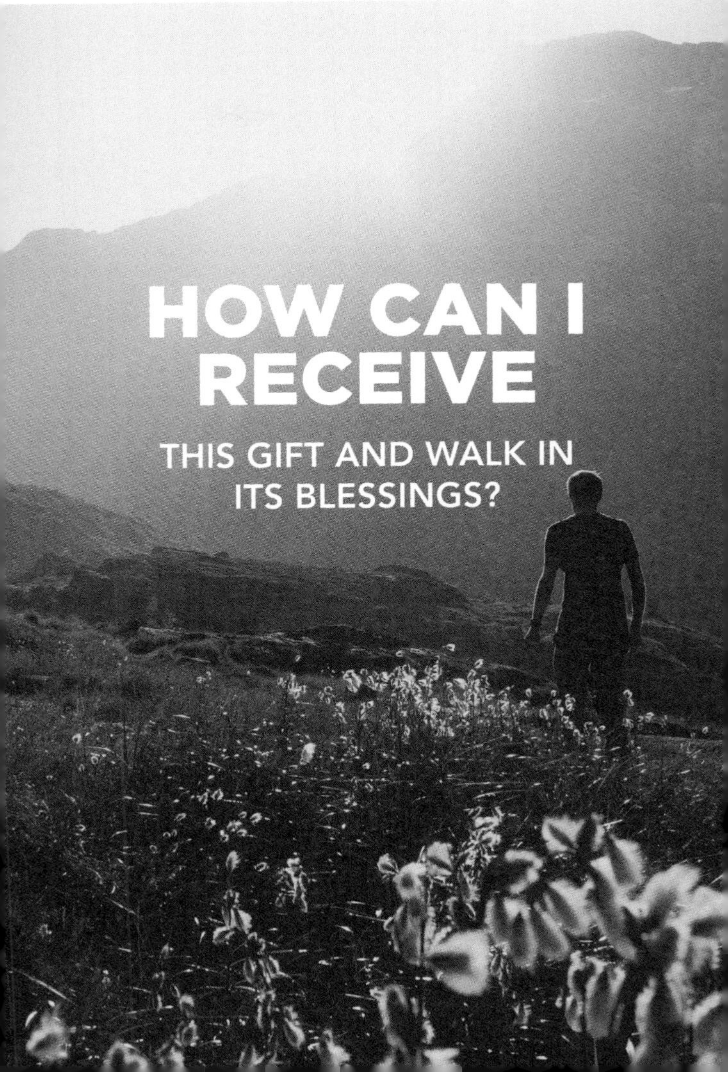

**Instead
of becoming
anxious
as you try
to handle
the situation
on your own,
pray in tongues
and experience
His rest.**

Beloved, tongues is God's precious grace gift to you. I hope you've seen through the Scriptures how it is one gift with many practical and powerful benefits.

If you are concerned about a matter today or looking to the Lord for wisdom or a breakthrough in any area of life, trust that the Spirit of God understands all your concerns, sees where the problem is, is able to heal you, and provide a heavenly answer better than what human might and smarts can come up with.

Instead of becoming anxious as you try to handle the situation in your own strength, I encourage you to pray in tongues. As you do, you're resting in the Lord's love and allowing Him to be God. He has promised that it is not by might nor by power, but *by His Spirit* that your mountain shall become a flat plain (see Zech. 4:6–7)!

Perhaps you already know how to pray in the Spirit, but for some time now, you've not practiced this wonderful grace gift. Can I encourage you to start doing it again? You will see His grace—His practical supply—invade every negative situation!

RECEIVE AND RELEASE YOUR HEAVENLY LANGUAGE

If you've never prayed or spoken in tongues before but would like to, let me lead you in a simple prayer to receive this gift. If you have made Jesus your Lord and Savior, rest assured you qualify for this gift.

Jesus Himself said, *"And these signs will follow those who believe: In My name they will...speak with new tongues"* (Mark 16:17). Do you believe in Jesus? Then you can be sure you will receive this gift when you ask in His name, for He also said:

"If you then, being evil, know how to give good gifts to your children, how much more will your heavenly Father give the Holy Spirit to those who ask Him!"

LUKE 11:11–13

Beloved, the Father, who's always ready to give good gifts to you, is more than ready to fill you with His Spirit and give you this heavenly language right now.

Are you ready? Lift up your hands to Him and say this with me:

Heavenly Father, I am confident that You will give me the baptism in the Holy Spirit with the ability to speak in tongues. Inundate me, fill me, and baptize me with the Holy Spirit. Jesus has paid the price for me to receive every blessing from You. So I receive right now Your Holy Spirit till overflowing and I fully expect to start speaking in my new heavenly language in Jesus' name. I will open my mouth and speak by faith right now. Thank You for all the benefits that praying in the Spirit will release in my life. In Jesus' name, Amen!

All right, now release your heavenly language. Go ahead and speak in tongues. Romans 8:26 tells us that the Holy Spirit helps us by making intercession for us.

The word "help" means "take hold together against" in Greek.[4] This means that the Holy Spirit takes hold of our problems together with us. He needs our participation. Exactly how do we participate? **We must open our mouths and give voice to Him.**

Some of you might feel like nothing happened. But once you have prayed asking God for the gift of tongues, know and believe that He is a God of His Word and has given you this gift simply because you asked Him for it (see Luke 11:13 again).

You may not have started speaking in tongues yet, but don't be discouraged. Begin by speaking the syllables that come to you. The Holy Spirit is not going to force you to speak. You need to cooperate with Him by opening your mouth and speaking in faith. When you are in church, ask someone you know who already speaks in tongues to pray with you. You can also pray in the Spirit as you worship the Lord in church or on your own.

And if at first, what you hear is monosyllabic, childlike sounds that differ from the tongues of other believers, don't be disheartened. Just keep at it. Spend some time praying in tongues each day and as you continue, what may have started off as a trickle will become a river. You will become more fluent in your new language, and the more you make praying in tongues part of your daily life, the more you will discover the inward peace, power, and sense of God's love that praying in the Spirit brings!

My friend, I pray you will experience a deeper walk with the Lord and see the miraculous manifesting in your life as you release His power through this wonderful gift of tongues!

Footnote:

4. NT: 4878, James Strong, *Biblesoft's New Exhaustive Strong's Numbers and Concordance with Expanded Greek-Hebrew Dictionary.* Copyright © 1994, 2003, 2006 Biblesoft, Inc. and International Bible Translators, Inc.

CLOSING WORDS

Beloved, God loves you so much He wants only what's best for you. That is why He gave you the gift of tongues. It is the prayer language He wants you to have because it will take your prayer life to a whole new level. Through this powerful gift, you can experience the love, power, and practical supply of the Holy Spirit supernaturally in your daily life.

Remember that because it is God's grace gift, all you need to do is ask Him for it and by faith, start praying in tongues. And if you already do pray in the Spirit, may you begin to make it a lifestyle—do it whenever and wherever you can. You don't need to switch your mind on for this, and life becomes a flow as you allow the Holy Spirit to work mightily in your circumstances.

I hope you've been blessed by the truths and testimonies I have shared in this book. If you would like to know more about the gift of tongues, I have shared more on the benefits and truths of the gift of tongues in other teaching resources.

Here are two of them that you can avail yourself of at JosephPrince.com:

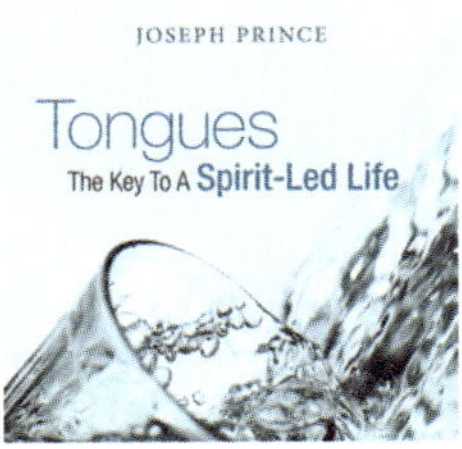

***TONGUES—THE KEY TO A SPIRIT-LED LIFE* (3-SERMON SERIES)**

***TONGUES—OUR GOD-GIVEN GIFT* (2-SERMON SERIES)**

And if you have been blessed by the testimonies in this book, do check out the Praise Reports page on my website for other inspiring stories.

May you find rivers of living water flowing abundantly in your life as you lay hold of the precious gift of tongues and begin an exciting, new journey of praying in the Spirit!

• • •

Special Appreciation

Special thanks and appreciation to all who have sent in their testimonies and praise reports to us. Kindly note that all testimonies are received in good faith and edited only for brevity and fluency. Names have been changed to protect the writers' privacy.

Salvation Prayer

If you would like to receive all that Jesus has done for you and make Him your Lord and Savior, please pray this prayer:

Lord Jesus, thank You for loving me and dying for me on the cross. Your precious blood washes me clean of every sin. You are my Lord and my Savior, now and forever. I believe You rose from the dead and that You are alive today. Because of Your finished work, I am now a beloved child of God and heaven is my home. Thank You for giving me eternal life and filling my heart with Your peace and joy. Amen.

We Would Like to Hear from You

If you have prayed the salvation prayer or if you have a testimony to share after reading this book, please tell us about it via JosephPrince.com/testimony. We'd love to hear from you!

Stay Connected with Joseph

Connect with Joseph through these social media channels and receive daily inspirational teachings:

Facebook.com/JosephPrince

Twitter.com/JosephPrince

Youtube.com/JosephPrinceOnline

Instagram: @JosephPrince

Free Daily E-mail Devotional

Sign up for Joseph's free daily e-mail devotional at JosephPrince.com/meditate and receive bite-size inspirations to help you grow in grace.

Other Books by Joseph Prince

Anchored

Live the Let-Go Life

Thoughts for Let-Go Living

The Prayer of Protection

Grace Revolution

The Power of Right Believing

Unmerited Favor

Destined to Reign

Healing Promises

Provision Promises

A Life Worth Living

The Benjamin Generation

Your Miracle Is in Your Mouth

Right Place Right Time

Spiritual Warfare

For more information on these books and other inspiring resources, visit JosephPrince.com.